" Happ
the new rich.
Inner peace is
the new success.
Health is the
new wealth.
Kindness is the new cool. "

Syed Balkhi

This journal belongs to:

Please Pirate this Challenge
Challenge no.100

Thank you for purchasing this journal!
This page is typically reserved for the copyright info in any book.

We really appreciate your purchase, and while we have tried to price this book affordably, we understand that there are those that may not be able to afford it.

We believe that having as many people as possible take part in the Practical Kindness Challenge will not only positively impact the world for the recipients of such kindness but also change the lives of the givers for the better too.

First Edition
Third Eye Press
Johannesburg
South Africa

Table of Contents

pg

Introduction

With this book, we aim to get people unstuck. In life, love and everything else that matters. Things rarely get better by us sitting around thinking about them from within the seemingly normal patterns of our lives. That's a long wait for a train that never comes. The world is out there. And while this may seem scary right now, this challenge aims to change that view by letting the world work for you, while you work for it.

This challenge can be a thrill ride, a treasure map, a way back home. Whatever it becomes for you, one thing is sure, it will change your perspective and multiply your gratitude exponentially for everything you are and everything you have. It helps you get unstuck by taking the guesswork out of what massive action you need to take – to put yourself out there, to make connections and seize opportunities that you otherwise would have never come across. To take all the good things we want to do for ourselves and others that are typically put off endlessly and shove them into today's to-do lists. Kindness Challenge, take the wheel!

By getting out there and practicing radical kindness, you CAN change the world into one that you fall more in love with every day, one act at a time. There is a magic hidden in kindness, compassion, and generosity that holds untold joy and unexpected, exponential benefits. All of which can only be unlocked by the (yet to be) version of you that stands on the other side of these completed challenges.

You won't look back, I promise.

The purpose of this journal:

- **Feel alive.** Experience the immediate boosts in mood, loving feelings, happiness, sense of purpose as well as the other health and wellness benefits associated with performing acts of kindness.

- **Grow through new experiences.** This journal will expose you to acts of kindness that you may never have thought of or thought yourself capable of and will help push you through discomfort to complete the challenges on the Bingo Board.

- **Gain lasting benefits.** Keep this journal as a record of your kind experiences that you can revisit time and time again. These will become your very own inspirational, feel-good short stories from your life. The last question on the challenge log pages will also let you see which acts of kindness you enjoy the most. This information could be used later on to select your favorite acts of kindness to do on an ongoing basis, for sustainable benefits for you and your loved ones.

- **Make the world kinder.** Your acts of kindness will inspire others to start doing the same. This kindness ripple effect works if you are the recipient of an act of kindness or even just a witness to a kind act, igniting the desire to pay it forward. You can also inspire others by posting your completed bingo board pics to your social media platforms and challenge others to play!

The Science of Kindness

Performing acts of kindness daily will reduce stress, anxiety, and depression. The body's of both the giver and the recipient of acts of kindness become filled with the same hormones, which make you more relaxed, healthier, and happier.

ENDORPHINS

✓ These are the brain's natural painkillers and are three times more effective than morphine.

SEROTONIN

✓ Heals your wounds.
✓ Calms you down.
✓ Makes you feel happy.

OXYTOCIN

✓ Reduces blood pressure.
✓ Strengthens the immune system.
✓ Has an immediate calming effect.
✓ Induces feelings of warmth, euphoria and connection to others, making you feel more loving and loved.

Studies have shown that people who practice kindness and compassion (e.g., give contributions of time or money) are 42% more likely to be happier than those who don't act kindly and compassionately toward others. They also have twice the amount of DHEA – which slows down aging and 23% less cortisol - the stress hormone.

Both the giver and receiver of kind actions will be more energized, feel fewer aches and pains, be more confident, and could even live longer.

Amazingly, the same benefits are experienced by those that witness random acts of kindness. People that see acts of generosity and compassion are inspired to follow suit and pay it forward, as they are filled with the same feel-good hormones. Kindness has a ripple effect!

https://www.randomactsofkindness.org

How to Use this Book

This journal contains 100 acts of kindness to complete.

1

PICK A KIND THING TO DO

- Read through the list and pick the acts that you think you can do first. Start off with something easy and work your way up to the acts that require more time/effort. The momentum you gain from completing challenges will help build the habit of kindness.

2

DO IT

- Each time you do a kind act on the list, complete the corresponding journal log entry for it soon after, while the event is still fresh in your memory.
- Tick off the challenge number on the relevant challenge index page as well as on the BINGO board.
    - o NOTE: These journal entries will become a record of the personal journey you go on, including its highs, lows, learnings and laughs along the way. The experiences that come out of this journey tend to be significant - this way, you can keep it with you for always.

Tick off challenge here

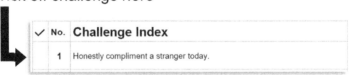

✓	No.	Challenge Index
	1	Honestly compliment a stranger today.

3

SHARE WHAT YOU DID TO INSPIRE OTHERS

- A complete row on the board wins!
- *Challenge no.98* - Once you complete a full row, snap a pic of your bingo board post this to your social media with the hashtag. #PracticalKindnessChallenge #Round1. You can repeat the process for every successful row and increment the hashtag to #Round2 for e.g.
- Once you've completed the whole BINGO board, post a pic and change the hashtag to #PracticalKindnessChallenge #Complete.

Some of these acts will take more bravery than you think, while others may seem small. But you'll be surprised at how massive the impact of a small act of kindness can be. Some things can be done quickly, while other items may depend on the right opportunity.

So what are you waiting for?

The Rules

1. All acts of kindness must be done in the spirit of giving and service with no expectation of return, for the benefits of the challenge to be maximized.
2. There is no time limit to the challenge. You can do things at your own pace and in your own time, but the idea is to create forward momentum, so try not to take too long between challenges.

Challenge modifications/exceptions

*   You may mark off items that you have already done in the past month before starting the challenge. If it's been longer than a month since you completed the act, then perform the act again. This is to ensure that your log entries are written from a fresh, vivid memory.

*   For the acts that ask if you have a partner where you are single, you can instead use a friend/family member.

*   Where you do not have kids, you can do the associated act of kindness with nieces/nephews or children of friends, where appropriate.

*   Where you do not think you can afford to complete an act of kindness that involves money, you may find a free/ homemade method to achieve the act that stays true to the spirit of the act.

*   For people whose parents have passed, you may complete such associated acts for any elders in your life that you love and respect.

*   Lastly, a particularly effective way to complete the challenge is to get a friend involved and start completing acts of kindness together – this will encourage accountability and keep the momentum going!

Challenge
BINGO BOARD

49	67	89	80	69	93	32	48	54	10
16	37	17	52	50	25	88	7	84	82
70	13	100	36	28	11	92	81	1	3
62	72	98	68	26	91	46	73	83	29
39	23	19	94	63	90	77	21	35	27
85	6	20	40	78	58	44	5	14	74
8	38	18	47	87	99	34	55	95	41
59	64	61	86	60	71	15	30	76	79
65	56	75	51	12	66	33	96	9	22
2	42	53	45	4	43	24	97	57	31

✓	No.	Challenge Index
	1	Give a stranger an honest compliment today.
	2	Donate your professional skills/talents to someone in need of them e.g. A photographer can provide a professional headshot for someone's CV.
	3	Leave kind/positive/motivational post-it notes on someone's car, in public bathrooms or on someone's desk.
	4	Pay for the person behind you in the queue. This could include things like coffee at a coffee shop, a toll, or bus fare.
	5	Social Media Challenge – People tend to only comment on the negative and neglect to comment on the positive – leave only kind comments on your chosen social media platforms for any of the people or group causes that you support for a week.
	6	Give your parents a call and tell them you love them. You may also do this for any elders that you love and respect in your life.
	7	Self Kindness – Show yourself some kindness by doing something that scares you, but builds you. e.g., contact that friend you've been avoiding, or go to that awesome gym class that you've been too afraid to try!
	8	Send a friend a handwritten letter about the positive impact they have on your life - deliberately take time to do this the long way.
	9	Volunteer for a day at a charity event/soup kitchen, etc.
	10	Go through your old clothes and donate any that you aren't using to those in need at a homeless shelter or The Salvation Army, e.g., warm clothes, shoes, and boots.
	11	Share word of mouth recommendations – If you know someone with exceptional professional skills, tell others eg., photography, art, babysitting, etc. Let others know. Take a few of their business cards to hand out to others that you know. People who work for themselves need word of mouth referrals.
	12	Ask a friend to do one random act of kindness from this list, for someone else.
	13	Let the person behind you in a queue, go first.
	14	Offer to get groceries for your friend/neighbor/relative who has a broken leg or other mobility problem.
	15	Call your in-laws just to say "Hi" and catch up.
	16	Message someone you love that you have not contacted in a while. Tell them that you love them.
	17	Try to find goodness in a person you don't like – write a list of ten good things about them.
	18	Tell your kids/nephews/nieces how talented your partner is at something.
	19	Compliment someone on their weight loss or tell them that they're "just glowing."
	20	Know anyone that's just had a baby or other major life event? – Offer to bring them a meal, clean up their house, or do a load of laundry for them.

✓	No.	Challenge Index
	21	Tell your boss how much you appreciate him/her and how much you've learned during the time that you've worked together.
	22	Social Media Challenge - Write a glowing recommendation on your chosen social media platform for all your friends/family that run small independent businesses.
	23	Buy a coffee for a co-worker that's having a rough day.
	24	Gift a book to a friend/family member from an online retailer as a surprise.
	25	Social Media Challenge - Go to your friends independent/small business social media pages, "like" their pages and share their services/ads for their businesses as a post to your profile to spread the word.
	26	Let someone else have your seat on a crowded bus, train, or waiting room.
	27	Create a happy scrapbook containing good memories and thoughts.
	28	Wash the car and/or fill up the gas tank for your partner and then leave their favorite snack on the dashboard for them to find in the morning before work.
	29	Tell your partner how amazingly beautiful they are when they are least expecting it.
	30	Buy something from a local maker/artisan.
	31	Offer to take a photo of a couple or for a tourist.
	32	Donate food to a homeless shelter.
	33	Leave a larger than average tip for hospitality staff /waitrons. Sign the receipt with a kind comment.
	34	Go through your kids' old clothes/toys/books and donate any that you aren't using to an orphanage. Old luggage is also useful.
	35	Help someone that seems lost – See tourists wandering around lost? Or someone walking around the office confused? Help them out and offer helpful suggestions from your experience.
	36	Offer to babysit a friend or family members kids for one day. This could be really appreciated if the parents are stressed or need to take some time for themselves.
	37	Thank your co-worker for doing a good job.
	38	Go to your friend's or family members kid's school/extracurricular/sports event to cheer them on.
	39	Self Kindness – Take a guilt free nap.
	40	Skype with the kids in your life that you don't get to see often – Kids love this and it gives them a chance to show off their latest creation or other things that they're proud of.

✓	No.	Challenge Index
	41	Keep a meal/snack/drinks in your car to give to a homeless person.
	42	Leave a loose note between the pages of a book/magazine with a positive message in it. This could be a library book that you return or one of your own that you donate to an old age home or just a magazine in a waiting room.
	43	Forgive someone that hurt you.
	44	Give your mother a thank-you card on your birthday. You can also do this for any parental figure in your life.
	45	Apologize to someone that you've hurt/mistreated.
	46	Take a friend up on an invitation to go out that you would usually decline, especially when you don't feel like it.
	47	Participate in a local event – The people who organize events always worry that no one will take part. e.g., Community book drive; yoga in the park; local bake-off.
	48	Self Kindness – Invest in your wellbeing - Schedule a full body massage/facial/yoga class/chiropractor session for yourself.
	49	If you know any friends/co-workers/acquaintances that will be alone during a holiday - invite them to join you for dinner.
	50	Listen to someone's long story/life story – Yes, the whole thing.
	51	Smile and have a friendly chit chat to anyone you wouldn't normally chat to - this could include a bus driver, barista, cleaning staff, etc.
	52	Make extra copies of photo printouts and send them to the people who are in those images. Sign the back of the photos with the names of the people in the picture and the date. People don't do this anymore which will make it extra special.
	53	Have you discovered product/service/knowledge/skill that has changed your life? – Share it on social media and inspire others to change their lives too.
	54	Hold a door open for someone to pass through first.
	55	Find a way to volunteer at a nursing home. Bake cookies for the elderly/play board games with them/play a musical instrument for them/read to them. Or just have a chat. You could make a new friend!
	56	Tell your partner's parents how skilled/amazing your partner is at something.
	57	Foster an animal. If you're able to, possibly adopt as well. But if you're not able to, then volunteer at an animal shelter.
	58	Donate food to an animal shelter.
	59	Bake a batch of cookies/cupcakes for your local fire or police station.
	60	Go through your household items and donate to those in need at homeless shelters or The Salvation Army. This can include old appliances/furniture/blankets etc. Or call the homeless shelter, ask what they need and take it to them.

✓	No.	Challenge Index
	61	Send a care package to someone who is away right now. This could be a person who is living/working far away or away in college.
	62	Cook someone a meal. Maybe you know someone who is having a hard time or is lonely? Doing this can mean a lot to someone.
	63	Tell someone's boss that you were given excellent service from an employee. Usually, hospitality/retail managers only hear negative comments, so going out of your way to say something positive is always a pleasure.
	64	Sponsor a family or buy gifts for the less fortunate for a holiday of your choice. Everyone in your family can contribute so that another family can enjoy that holiday as well.
	65	Create a ready-to-go bag for someone that is less fortunate than you are. You can help the homeless by filling a bag with a bottle of water, a quick snack (e.g., raisins), gloves, toothpaste & toothbrush, small packets of dog food (their dogs are hungry too!), etc.
	66	Notice someone's kid being well-behaved? – Tell their parents how good they are in front of the kid. It will encourage the child to continue being good and will make the parents feel proud as well.
	67	Do a favor for someone randomly and without expectation.
	68	Allow your partner/family member to sleep in while you make them breakfast in bed.
	69	Don't complain/pass negative comments about anything for a whole day.
	70	Write a list of things that you love about a friend then send it to them.
	71	Send coloring books to sick kids in the hospital.
	72	Donate books that you don't need anymore. You can donate to libraries, hospitals, nursing homes, etc.
	73	For your next birthday, ask everyone to donate to a charity for you, instead of buying presents.
	74	Write a list of things you love about your partner/family member and give it to them.
✓	75	Draw a happy image on the ground in chalk on the sidewalk. e.g., smiley face with the note "You are amazing!"/"The world needs you!"
	76	Social Media Challenge - Give a glowing recommendation for at least 3 locally run restaurants where you love to eat on Facebook/Yelp (or any similar food review app).
	77	Write a letter or email someone (teacher, parent, leader, etc.) that has made a difference in your life and thank them.
	78	Participate in a fundraising event at your local school/community hall.
	79	Tell your partner what a good hair/butt day they're having.
	80	Self Kindness - Take yourself on a date. Go see a movie or eat a special meal at a restaurant.

✓	No.	Challenge Index
	81	Do a chore that you usually don't do for your partner/family member/roommate. This could include doing the dishes, cleaning your home, taking out the trash, making a meal, dealing with a bill, etc.
	82	Bring your own sustainable, reusable bags to the mall so that the stores don't have to pack your purchased items in plastic bags, which are bad for the environment.
	83	Bring donuts or other delicious sweets (homemade or store-bought) to work for your co-workers on a random Monday.
	84	Plant a vegetable garden in your community garden or your own backyard.
	85	Avoid gossip - turn down a negative gossip situation and say something nice about the person instead.
	86	Give the painter/electrician/handyman a glass of ice cold water/cold soda/hot coffee, while they are on the job at your house.
	87	Self Kindness - Get up early enough to mindfully watch and appreciate the sunrise.
	88	Donate blood.
	89	Plant a tree.
	90	If you see a parking meter about to expire, put some spare change in it. Or leave change in the coin return slot of parking ticket pay station.
	91	Give someone that's having a rough day a hug.
	92	Pick up litter you see on the side of the sidewalk or bring a trash bag when you go for a walk and collect any trash that you may come across.
	93	Leave coupons on staple/essential food items on the shelf at the grocery store for others to use.
	94	Give a handmade gift to a friend.
	95	If you have a wedding or a party, donate your decorations and flowers to a hospital or a nursing home afterward. You can also give any extra party decorations you may have in storage.
	96	Bring a security guard a hot cup of coffee.
	97	Clean up litter at a local communal garden/park area.
	98	Tag others - Post a pic of your winning bingo board page every time you complete a row to your social media along with the hashtag: **#PracticalKindnessChallenge #Round(X)** to inspire others to try the challenge and spread more random acts of kindness!
	99	Recommend this book to others - If you enjoyed this challenge and it made a positive impact on your life, please leave a review on Amazon for this book.
	100	Pirate this challenge - Recommend this challenge to a friend or family member that you think needs to experience the Practical Kindness Challenge. We encourage you to photocopy the bingo board page as well as the rules and index pages containing the 100 challenges so that you can pass this on without having to buy this journal.

Happiness is the only good. The time to be happy is now. The place to be happy is here. The way to be happy is to make others so.

Robert Green Ingersoll

Give a stranger an honest compliment today.

Date/Time/Place:

What did you do?

What did it make you feel?

What did you learn?

Would you do this again?   YES / NO

Donate your professional skills/talents to someone in need of them e.g. A photographer can provide a professional headshot for someone's CV.

Date/Time/Place:

What did you do?

What did it make you feel?

What did you learn?

Would you do this again?   YES / NO

Leave kind/positive/motivational post-it notes on someone's car, in public bathrooms or on someone's desk.

Date/Time/Place:

What did you do?

What did it make you feel?

What did you learn?

Would you do this again?   YES / NO

Pay for the person behind you in the queue. This could include things like coffee at a coffee shop, a toll, or bus fare.

Date/Time/Place:

What did you do?

What did it make you feel?

What did you learn?

Would you do this again? YES / NO

Social Media Challenge – People tend to only comment on the negative and neglect to comment on the positive – leave only kind comments on your chosen social media platforms for any of the people or group causes that you support for a week.

Date/Time/Place:

What did you do?

What did it make you feel?

What did you learn?

Would you do this again?   YES / NO

Give your parents a call and tell them you love them. You may also do this for any elders that you love and respect in your life.

Date/Time/Place:

What did you do?

What did it make you feel?

What did you learn?

Would you do this again?   YES / NO

Self Kindness – Show yourself some kindness by doing something that scares you, but builds you. e.g., contact that friend you've been avoiding, or go to that awesome gym class that you've been too afraid to try!

Date/Time/Place:

What did you do?

What did it make you feel?

What did you learn?

Would you do this again?   YES / NO

"The stranger who receives the rare gift of human kindness holds its value in his heart forever.

———————

Charles Dudley Warner

Send a friend a handwritten letter about the positive impact they have on your life - deliberately take time to do this the long way.

Date/Time/Place:

What did you do?

What did it make you feel?

What did you learn?

Would you do this again?   YES / NO

Volunteer for a day at a charity event/soup kitchen, etc.

Date/Time/Place:

What did you do?

What did it make you feel?

What did you learn?

Would you do this again?   YES / NO

Go through your old clothes and donate any that you aren't using to those in need at a homeless shelter or The Salvation Army, e.g., warm clothes, shoes, and boots.

Date/Time/Place:

What did you do?

What did it make you feel?

What did you learn?

Would you do this again?   YES / NO

Share word of mouth recommendations – If you know someone with exceptional professional skills, tell others eg., photography, art, babysitting, etc. Let others know. Take a few of their business cards to hand out to others that you know. People who work for themselves need word of mouth referrals.

Date/Time/Place:

What did you do?

What did it make you feel?

What did you learn?

Would you do this again?   YES / NO

Ask a friend to do one random act of kindness from this list, for someone else.

Date/Time/Place:

What did you do?

What did it make you feel?

What did you learn?

Would you do this again?   YES / NO

Let the person behind you in a queue, go first.

Date/Time/Place:

....

....

What did you do?

....

....

....

....

....

....

....

....

....

....

What did it make you feel?

....

....

What did you learn?

....

....

....

....

Would you do this again?   YES / NO

Offer to get groceries for your friend/neighbor/relative who has a broken leg or other mobility problem.

Date/Time/Place:

What did you do?

What did it make you feel?

What did you learn?

Would you do this again?   YES / NO

Call your in-laws just to say "Hi" and catch up.

Date/Time/Place:

What did you do?

What did it make you feel?

What did you learn?

Would you do this again?   YES / NO

Message someone you love that you have not contacted in a while. Tell them that you love them.

Date/Time/Place:

What did you do?

What did it make you feel?

What did you learn?

Would you do this again?   YES / NO

Try to find goodness in a person you don't like – write a list of ten good things about them.

Date/Time/Place:

What did you do?

What did it make you feel?

What did you learn?

Would you do this again?   YES / NO

Tell your kids/nephews/nieces how talented your partner is at something.

Date/Time/Place:

What did you do?

What did it make you feel?

What did you learn?

Would you do this again?   YES / NO

Compliment someone on their weight loss or tell them that they're "just glowing."

Date/Time/Place:

What did you do?

What did it make you feel?

What did you learn?

Would you do this again?   YES / NO

Know anyone that's just had a baby or other major life event? –
Offer to bring them a meal, clean up their house, or do a load of
laundry for them.

Date/Time/Place:

What did you do?

What did it make you feel?

What did you learn?

Would you do this again?   YES / NO

Tell your boss how much you appreciate him/her and how much you've learned during the time that you've worked together.

Date/Time/Place:

What did you do?

What did it make you feel?

What did you learn?

Would you do this again?   YES / NO

"No act of kindness – no matter how small – *is ever wasted.*"

———

AESOP

Social Media Challenge - Write a glowing recommendation on your chosen social media platforms for all your friends/family that run small independent businesses.

Date/Time/Place:

What did you do?

What did it make you feel?

What did you learn?

Would you do this again?   YES / NO

Buy a coffee for a co-worker that's having a rough day.

Date/Time/Place:

What did you do?

What did it make you feel?

What did you learn?

Would you do this again?   YES / NO

Gift a book to a friend/family member from an online retailer as a surprise.

Date/Time/Place:

What did you do?

What did it make you feel?

What did you learn?

Would you do this again?   YES / NO

Social Media Challenge - Go to your friends independent/small business social media pages, "like" their pages and share their services/ads for their businesses as a post to your profile to spread the word.

Date/Time/Place:

What did you do?

What did it make you feel?

What did you learn?

Would you do this again?   YES / NO

Let someone else have your seat on a crowded bus, train, or waiting room.

Date/Time/Place:

What did you do?

What did it make you feel?

What did you learn?

Would you do this again?   YES / NO

Create a happy scrapbook containing good memories and thoughts.

Date/Time/Place:

What did you do?

What did it make you feel?

What did you learn?

Would you do this again?   YES / NO

Wash the car and/or fill up the gas tank for your partner and then leave their favorite snack on the dashboard for them to find in the morning before work.

Date/Time/Place:

What did you do?

What did it make you feel?

What did you learn?

Would you do this again?   YES / NO

The various features and aspects of human life, such as longevity, good health, success, happiness, and so forth, which we consider desirable, are all dependent on kindness and a good heart...

Dalai Lama

Tell your partner how amazingly beautiful they are when they are least expecting it.

Date/Time/Place:

What did you do?

What did it make you feel?

What did you learn?

Would you do this again?   YES / NO

Buy something from a local maker/artisan.

Date/Time/Place:

What did you do?

What did it make you feel?

What did you learn?

Would you do this again?   YES / NO

Offer to take a photo of a couple or for a tourist.

Date/Time/Place:

What did you do?

What did it make you feel?

What did you learn?

Would you do this again?   YES / NO

Donate food to a homeless shelter.

Date/Time/Place:

What did you do?

What did it make you feel?

What did you learn?

Would you do this again?   YES / NO

Leave a larger than average tip for hospitality staff /waitrons. Sign the receipt with a kind comment.

Date/Time/Place:

What did you do?

What did it make you feel?

What did you learn?

Would you do this again?   YES / NO

Go through your kids' old clothes/toys/books and donate any that you aren't using to an orphanage. Old luggage is also useful.

Date/Time/Place:

What did you do?

What did it make you feel?

What did you learn?

Would you do this again?   YES / NO

Help someone that seems lost – See tourists wandering around lost? Or someone walking around the office confused? Help them out and offer helpful suggestions from your experience.

Date/Time/Place:

What did you do?

What did it make you feel?

What did you learn?

Offer to babysit a friend or family members kids for one day. This could be really appreciated if the parents are stressed or need to take some time for themselves.

Date/Time/Place:

What did you do?

What did it make you feel?

What did you learn?

Would you do this again?   YES / NO

Thank your co-worker for doing a good job.

Date/Time/Place:

What did you do?

What did it make you feel?

What did you learn?

Would you do this again?   YES / NO

Go to your friend's or family members kid's
school/extracurricular/sports event to cheer them on.

Date/Time/Place:

What did you do?

What did it make you feel?

What did you learn?

Would you do this again?   YES / NO

Self Kindness – Take a guilt free nap.

Date/Time/Place:

What did you do?

What did it make you feel?

What did you learn?

Would you do this again?   YES / NO

Skype with the kids in your life that you don't get to see often – Kids love this and it gives them a chance to show off their latest creation or other things that they're proud of.

Date/Time/Place:

What did you do?

What did it make you feel?

What did you learn?

Would you do this again?   YES / NO

Keep a meal/snack/drinks in your car to give to a homeless person.

Date/Time/Place:

What did you do?

What did it make you feel?

What did you learn?

Would you do this again?   YES / NO

Leave a loose note between the pages of a book/magazine with a positive message in it. This could be a library book that you return or one of your own that you donate to an old age home or just a magazine in a waiting room.

Date/Time/Place:

What did you do?

What did it make you feel?

What did you learn?

Would you do this again?   YES / NO

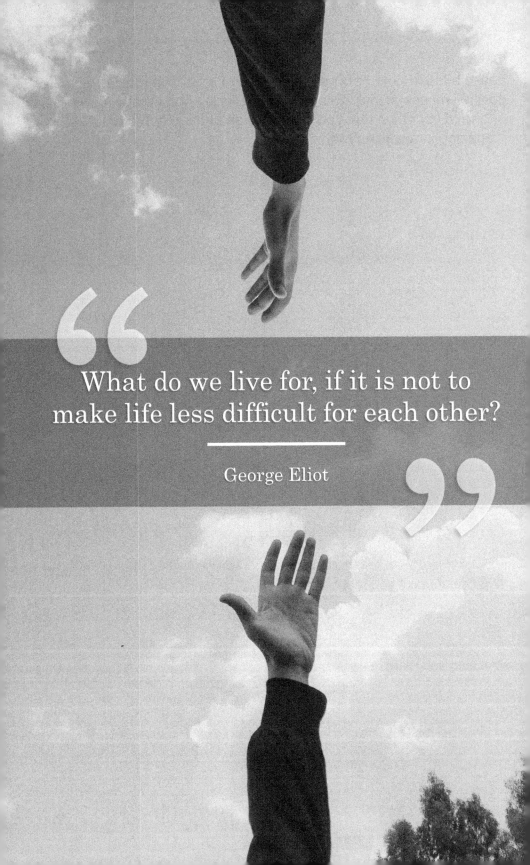

> "What do we live for, if it is not to make life less difficult for each other?"
>
> George Eliot

Forgive someone that hurt you.

Date/Time/Place:

What did you do?

What did it make you feel?

What did you learn?

Would you do this again?   YES / NO

Give your mother a thank-you card on your birthday. You can also do this for any parental figure in your life.

Date/Time/Place:

What did you do?

What did it make you feel?

What did you learn?

Would you do this again?   YES / NO

Apologize to someone that you've hurt/mistreated.

Date/Time/Place:

What did you do?

What did it make you feel?

What did you learn?

Would you do this again?   YES / NO

Take a friend up on an invitation to go out that you would usually decline, especially when you don't feel like it.

Date/Time/Place:

What did you do?

What did it make you feel?

What did you learn?

Would you do this again?   YES / NO

Participate in a local event – The people who organize events always worry that no one will take part. e.g., Community book drive; yoga in the park; local bake-off.

Date/Time/Place:

What did you do?

What did it make you feel?

What did you learn?

Would you do this again?   YES / NO

Self Kindness – Invest in your wellbeing - Schedule a full body massage/facial/yoga class/chiropractor session for yourself.

Date/Time/Place:

What did you do?

What did it make you feel?

What did you learn?

Would you do this again?   YES / NO

If you know any friends/co-workers/acquaintances that will be alone during a holiday - invite them to join you for dinner.

Date/Time/Place:

What did you do?

What did it make you feel?

What did you learn?

Would you do this again?   YES / NO

"Kindness in words creates confidence. Kindness in thinking creates profoundness. *Kindness in giving creates love.*

———

Lao Tzu

Listen to someone's long story/life story – Yes, the whole thing.

Date/Time/Place:

What did you do?

What did it make you feel?

What did you learn?

Would you do this again?   YES / NO

Smile and have a friendly chit chat to anyone you wouldn't normally chat to - this could include a bus driver, barista, cleaning staff, etc.

Date/Time/Place:

What did you do?

What did it make you feel?

What did you learn?

Would you do this again?   YES / NO

Make extra copies of photo printouts and send them to the people who are in those images. Sign the back of the photos with the names of the people in the picture and the date. People don't do this anymore which will make it extra special.

Date/Time/Place:

What did you do?

What did it make you feel?

What did you learn?

Would you do this again?   YES / NO

Have you discovered product/service/knowledge/skill that has changed your life? – Share it on social media and inspire others to change their lives too.

Date/Time/Place:

What did you do?

What did it make you feel?

What did you learn?

Would you do this again?   YES / NO

Hold a door open for someone to pass through first.

Date/Time/Place:

What did you do?

What did it make you feel?

What did you learn?

Would you do this again?   YES / NO

Find a way to volunteer at a nursing home. Bake cookies for the elderly/play board games with them/play a musical instrument for them/read to them. Or just have a chat. You could make a new friend!

Date/Time/Place:

What did you do?

What did it make you feel?

What did you learn?

Would you do this again?   YES / NO

Tell your partner's parents how skilled/amazing your partner is at something.

Date/Time/Place:

What did you do?

What did it make you feel?

What did you learn?

Would you do this again?   YES / NO

Foster an animal. If you're able to, possibly adopt as well. But if you're not able to, then volunteer at an animal shelter.

Date/Time/Place:

What did you do?

What did it make you feel?

What did you learn?

Would you do this again?   YES / NO

Donate food to an animal shelter.

Date/Time/Place:

What did you do?

What did it make you feel?

What did you learn?

Would you do this again?   YES / NO

Bake a batch of cookies/cupcakes for your local fire or police station.

Date/Time/Place:

What did you do?

What did it make you feel?

What did you learn?

Would you do this again?   YES / NO

Go through your household items and donate to those in need at homeless shelters or The Salvation Army. This can include old appliances/furniture/blankets etc. Or call the homeless shelter, ask what they need and take it to them.

Date/Time/Place:

What did you do?

What did it make you feel?

What did you learn?

Would you do this again?   YES / NO

Send a care package to someone who is away right now. This could be a person who is living/working far away or away in college.

Date/Time/Place:

What did you do?

What did it make you feel?

What did you learn?

Would you do this again?   YES / NO

Cook someone a meal. Maybe you know someone who is having a hard time or is lonely? Doing this can mean a lot to someone.

Date/Time/Place:

What did you do?

What did it make you feel?

What did you learn?

Would you do this again?   YES / NO

Tell someone's boss that you were given excellent service from an employee. Usually, hospitality/retail managers only hear negative comments, so going out of your way to say something positive is always a pleasure.

Date/Time/Place:

What did you do?

What did it make you feel?

What did you learn?

Would you do this again?   YES / NO

" The world is full of
kind people...
If you can't find
one, *be one*. "

———

Unknown

Sponsor a family or buy gifts for the less fortunate for a holiday of your choice. Everyone in your family can contribute so that another family can enjoy that holiday as well.

Date/Time/Place:

What did you do?

What did it make you feel?

What did you learn?

Would you do this again?   YES / NO

Create a ready-to-go bag for someone that is less fortunate than you are. You can help the homeless by filling a bag with a bottle of water, a quick snack (e.g., raisins), gloves, toothpaste & toothbrush, small packets of dog food (their dogs are hungry too!), etc.

Date/Time/Place:

What did you do?

What did it make you feel?

What did you learn?

Would you do this again?   YES / NO

Notice someone's kid being well-behaved? – Tell their parents how good they are in front of the kid. It will encourage the child to continue being good and will make the parents feel proud as well.

Date/Time/Place:

What did you do?

What did it make you feel?

What did you learn?

Would you do this again?   YES / NO

Do a favor for someone randomly and without expectation.

Date/Time/Place:

What did you do?

What did it make you feel?

What did you learn?

Would you do this again?   YES / NO

Allow your partner/family member to sleep in while you make them breakfast in bed.

Date/Time/Place:

What did you do?

What did it make you feel?

What did you learn?

Would you do this again?   YES / NO

Don't complain/pass negative comments about anything for a whole day.

Date/Time/Place:

What did you do?

What did it make you feel?

What did you learn?

Would you do this again?   YES / NO

Write a list of things that you love about a friend then send it to them.

Date/Time/Place:

What did you do?

What did it make you feel?

What did you learn?

Would you do this again?   YES / NO

"You cannot do a kindness too soon, *for you never know how soon it will be too late.*

Ralph Waldo Emerson

Send coloring books to sick kids in the hospital.

Date/Time/Place:

What did you do?

What did it make you feel?

What did you learn?

Would you do this again?   YES / NO

Donate books that you don't need anymore. You can donate to libraries, hospitals, nursing homes, etc.

Date/Time/Place:

What did you do?

What did it make you feel?

What did you learn?

Would you do this again?   YES / NO

For your next birthday, ask everyone to donate to a charity for you, instead of buying presents.

Date/Time/Place:

What did you do?

What did it make you feel?

What did you learn?

Would you do this again?   YES / NO

Write a list of things you love about your partner/family member and give it to them.

Date/Time/Place:

What did you do?

What did it make you feel?

What did you learn?

Would you do this again?   YES / NO

Draw a happy image on the ground in chalk on the sidewalk. e.g., smiley face with the note "You are amazing!"/"The world needs you!"

Date/Time/Place:

What did you do?

What did it make you feel?

What did you learn?

Would you do this again?   YES / NO

Social Media Challenge - Give a glowing recommendation for at least 3 locally run restaurants where you love to eat on Facebook/Yelp (or any similar food review app).

Date/Time/Place:

What did you do?

What did it make you feel?

What did you learn?

Would you do this again?   YES / NO

Write a letter or email someone (teacher, parent, leader, etc.) that has made a difference in your life and thank them.

Date/Time/Place:

What did you do?

What did it make you feel?

What did you learn?

Would you do this again?   YES / NO

Participate in a fundraising event at your local school/community hall.

Date/Time/Place:

What did you do?

What did it make you feel?

What did you learn?

Would you do this again?   YES / NO

Tell your partner what a good hair/butt day they're having.

Date/Time/Place:

What did you do?

What did it make you feel?

What did you learn?

Would you do this again?   YES / NO

Self Kindness - Take yourself on a date. Go see a movie or eat a special meal at a restaurant.

Date/Time/Place:

What did you do?

What did it make you feel?

What did you learn?

Would you do this again?   YES / NO

Do a chore that you usually don't do for your partner/family member/roommate. This could include doing the dishes, cleaning your home, taking out the trash, making a meal, dealing with a bill, etc.

Date/Time/Place:

What did you do?

What did it make you feel?

What did you learn?

Would you do this again?   YES / NO

Bring your own sustainable, reusable bags to the mall so that the stores don't have to pack your purchased items in plastic bags, which are bad for the environment.

Date/Time/Place:

What did you do?

What did it make you feel?

What did you learn?

Would you do this again?   YES / NO

Bring donuts or other delicious sweets (homemade or store-bought) to work for your co-workers on a random Monday.

Date/Time/Place:

What did you do?

What did it make you feel?

What did you learn?

Would you do this again?   YES / NO

Plant a vegetable garden in your community garden or your own backyard.

Date/Time/Place:

What did you do?

What did it make you feel?

What did you learn?

Would you do this again?   YES / NO

I expect to pass through life but once. If therefore, there be any kindness I can show, or any good thing I can do to any fellow being, *let me do it now, and not defer or neglect it, as I shall not pass this way again.*

———————

William Penn

Avoid gossip - turn down a negative gossip situation and say something nice about the person instead.

Date/Time/Place:

What did you do?

What did it make you feel?

What did you learn?

Would you do this again?   YES / NO

Give the painter/electrician/handyman a glass of ice cold water/cold soda/hot coffee, while they are on the job at your house.

Date/Time/Place:

What did you do?

What did it make you feel?

What did you learn?

Would you do this again?   YES / NO

Self Kindness - Get up early enough to mindfully watch and appreciate the sunrise.

Date/Time/Place:

What did you do?

What did it make you feel?

What did you learn?

Would you do this again?   YES / NO

Donate blood.

Date/Time/Place:

What did you do?

What did it make you feel?

What did you learn?

Would you do this again?   YES / NO

Plant a tree.

Date/Time/Place:

What did you do?

What did it make you feel?

What did you learn?

Would you do this again?   YES / NO

If you see a parking meter about to expire, put some spare change in it. Or leave change in the coin return slot of parking ticket pay station.

Date/Time/Place:

What did you do?

What did it make you feel?

What did you learn?

Would you do this again?   YES / NO

Give someone that's having a rough day a hug.

Date/Time/Place:

What did you do?

What did it make you feel?

What did you learn?

Would you do this again?   YES / NO

" How beautiful a day can be
when kindness touches it...

———

George Elliston

Pick up litter you see on the side of the sidewalk or bring a trash bag when you go for a walk and collect any trash that you may come across.

Date/Time/Place:

What did you do?

What did it make you feel?

What did you learn?

Would you do this again?   YES / NO

Leave coupons on staple/essential food items on the shelf at the grocery store for others to use.

Date/Time/Place:

What did you do?

What did it make you feel?

What did you learn?

Would you do this again?   YES / NO

Give a handmade gift to a friend.

Date/Time/Place:

What did you do?

What did it make you feel?

What did you learn?

Would you do this again?   YES / NO

If you have a wedding or a party, donate your decorations and flowers to a hospital or a nursing home afterward. You can also give any extra party decorations you may have in storage.

Date/Time/Place:

What did you do?

What did it make you feel?

What did you learn?

Would you do this again?   YES / NO

Bring a security guard a hot cup of coffee.

Date/Time/Place:

What did you do?

What did it make you feel?

What did you learn?

Would you do this again?   YES / NO

Clean up litter at a local communal garden/park area.

Date/Time/Place:

What did you do?

What did it make you feel?

What did you learn?

Would you do this again?   YES / NO

Tag others - Post a pic of your winning bingo board page every time you complete a row to your social media along with the hashtag: **#PracticalKindnessChallenge #Round(X)** to inspire others to try the challenge and spread more random acts of kindness!

Date/Time/Place:

What did you do?

What did it make you feel?

What did you learn?

Would you do this again?   YES / NO

Recommend this book to others - If you enjoyed this challenge and it made a positive impact on your life, please leave a review on Amazon for this book.

Date/Time/Place:

What did you do?

What did it make you feel?

What did you learn?

Would you do this again?   YES / NO

Pirate this challenge - Recommend this challenge to a friend or family member that you think needs to experience the Practical Kindness Challenge. We encourage you to photocopy the bingo board page as well as the rules and index pages containing the 100 challenges so that you can pass this on without having to buy this journal.

Date/Time/Place:

What did you do?

What did it make you feel?

What did you learn?

Would you do this again?   YES / NO

Your own kind act here:

Date/Time/Place:

What did you do?

What did it make you feel?

What did you learn?

Would you do this again?   YES / NO

Your own kind act here:

Date/Time/Place:

What did you do?

What did it make you feel?

What did you learn?

Would you do this again?   YES / NO

Your own kind act here:

Date/Time/Place:

What did you do?

What did it make you feel?

What did you learn?

Would you do this again?   YES / NO

Your own kind act here:

Date/Time/Place:

What did you do?

What did it make you feel?

What did you learn?

Would you do this again?   YES / NO

Your own kind act here:

Date/Time/Place:

What did you do?

What did it make you feel?

What did you learn?

Would you do this again?   YES / NO

OVERALL CHALLENGE REVIEW

Do you feel that your life and overall happiness
have improved through the challenge? And if so, how?

....

....

....

....

....

....

....

Name three things that you enjoyed most about the challenge:

....

....

....

....

....

....

List three important learnings that were the highlights of this
challenge for you:

....

....

....

....

....

....

Thank you for being you.

Well done on making the world a better place!
We are 100% sure that completing the Practical Kindness
Challenge has had massive positive impacts on the overall
quality of your life, your health, your loved ones, and maybe
even your business! Your fantastic journey will always be
right here in this book for you to reflect on anytime.

But please remember that you don't have to stop here – you
can redo this challenge anytime, especially the ones that you
most enjoyed! Each time you repeat these random acts of
kindness, it will produce unique, joyful experiences.
You can also Challenge others to try it out and keep the
kindness chain reaction going!

So keep being amazing.
The world needs you.

If you found value in this book, please consider leaving a
review on Amazon, it would be much appreciated and would
help us improve future versions of the book.
Challenge no. 99

THE LITTLE
THINGS
MATTER

RECOMMENDED BOOKS

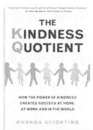

The Kindness Quotient:
How the Power of Kindness Creates Success at Home, At Work and in the World
Author: Rhonda Sciortino

KQ, or kindness quotient, is a measure of how much each of us embodies the virtues of kindness, caring and generosity. A high KQ means taking advantage of all opportunities to be kind and finding personal success by bringing kindness into the world. Now there's a way to boost your KQ and maximize your kindness potential.

Chicken Soup for the Soul: Random Acts of Kindness:
101 Stories of Compassion and Paying It Forward
Author: Amy Newmark

Small gestures can make a big difference in someone's day, even someone's life. This collection of 101 uplifting, true stories will help you see the beauty in small, meaningful gestures and how such acts can make a difference in someone else's life. From random acts of kindness to doing what's right, this book shows how positive attitudes and good deeds can change the world.

The War for Kindness:
Building Empathy in a Fractured World
Author: Jamil Zaki

"Beautifully written and deeply felt, *The War for Kindness* is an outstanding scientific analysis of our species' best and last hope for survival—our unique ability to care about each other."—**Daniel Gilbert, author of *Stumbling on Happiness***

Go Be Kind:
28 1/2 Adventures Guaranteed to Make You Happier
Author: Leon Logothetis

Go Be Kind isn't just a journal or another how-to guide to creating the life you want. It's a series of daily adventures that will help you rediscover the greatest human gift—kindness, which inspires interpersonal connection and is the most rewarding way to lead a more magnificent life.

The Kindness Diaries:
One Man's Quest to Ignite Goodwill and Transform Lives Around the World
Author: Leon Logothetis

The incredible journey of one man who sets out to circumnavigate the globe on a vintage motorbike fueled by kindness.

RECOMMENDED WEBSITES

www.randomactsofkindness.org
We are rooted in the belief that all people can connect through kindness and that kindness can be taught. We follow a simple framework for everything we do.
Inspire -> Empower -> Act -> Reflect -> Share. Our evidence-based Kindness in the Classroom® curriculum gives students the social and emotional skills needed to live more successful lives. Our workplace kindness calendar shows companies how easy it is to change workplace culture through simple kind gestures. We create a common language between schools, work and home with all of our resources.

www.kindness.org/
We are a nonprofit with a bold hypothesis: Kindness is the catalyst in solving the world's biggest challenges. We believe a kinder world is possible, and we're here to make it happen.

www.thegreatkindnesschallenge.com
The Great Kindness Challenge is proudly presented by Kids for Peace, a global 501(c)(3) nonprofit organization. Kids for Peace was co-founded in 2006 by Danielle Gram, a high school honors student and Jill McManigal, a mother and former elementary school teacher. What started organically as a neighborhood group of kids wanting to make our world a better place, has grown into an interconnected network of young peacebuilders worldwide.

Made in the USA
Coppell, TX
05 March 2024

29775150R00075